THE YEAR THE GIANTS
WON THE SERIES

OTHER BOOKS BY JOSEPH SUTTON

Fiction

A Class of Leaders

Morning Pages: The Almost True Story of My Life

Highway Sailor: A Rollicking American Journey

The Immortal Mouth and Other Stories

Nonfiction

Write Now! On the Road to Getting Published or How I Learned to Sell My Book

Words of Wellness: A Treasury of Quotations for Well-Being

My Writing Year: Making Sense of Being a Writer

THE YEAR THE GIANTS WON THE SERIES

A Journal of the
2010 World Series Champions

Joseph Sutton

Mad Dog
PUBLISHING COMPANY

For information contact:
Mad Dog Publishing Co.
joe@joesutt.com, www.joesutt.com
www.authorconnect.com

Illustrations © 2011 by Donald S. Ellis

ISBN Number: 978-0-9825598-4-0
Printed in the United States of America

Cover Art: "The Freak" (Tim Lincecum) courtesy of artist Robert Marosi Bustamante and the George Krevsky Gallery, San Francisco.

To my son Ray, a GIANT Giants fan.

Joseph Sutton with his son Ray after the
2010 Giants World Series Victory Parade.

Vs. Phillies, Game 1: Cody Ross

Cody, Cody,

Bang, Bang.

> — Steve Hermanos, from
> *O, Gigantic Victory!*

THE YEAR THE GIANTS WON THE SERIES

Preface

One August evening, soon after I moved to San Francisco in 1978, I went to a night game at Candlestick Park between the Giants and their archrivals, the L.A. Dodgers. Because I grew up in Los Angeles I was a longtime Dodger rooter. By the end of the game, though, my thought processes had changed. The way the Giants came back to win the game was part of what altered my thinking. The most bizarre play I've ever witnessed in a baseball game took place on that chilly evening. The Dodgers were a run behind when they came to bat in the top of the ninth. With two outs, the bases empty, Lee Lacy of the Dodgers hit a line drive to right center field. Jack Clark in right and Larry Herndon in center both started for the ball at full speed. They were headed for each other when CRASH, they collided and crumpled to the ground. Herndon actually caught the ball, but while he and Clark were writhing in pain on the ground, the ball rolled out of his glove. Lacy rounded the bases for an inside the park home run to tie the game. Although momentum was on the Dodgers' side, the Giants came right back in the bottom of the ninth to score the winning run, making 50,000 Giants fans go absolutely wild with joy.

But the main reason I became a Giants fan was because it dawned on me that if I was going to live in San Francisco for the rest of my life, I might as well root, root, root for the home team.

I've been doing it ever since.

Because the Giants were such an exciting team, I kept a journal, starting in June, of their

2010 season. Little did I know they would soar to the heights of the baseball world. They didn't have any superstars except for maybe two-time Cy Young winner Tim Lincecum, also known as "The Freak" due to his shaggy long hair, slim build (5'11", 160 lbs.), his pitching velocity and an unorthodox pitching style. The Giants' roster was made up of a bunch of ragtag ballplayers. But you could see the effort they expended in every game. They had a never-say-die attitude that was evident to everyone in Giantsland. This was definitely my kind of team. And this is how they endeared themselves, not only to me, but to all their loyal followers.

This book is not only about the Giants' 2010 world championship season, it's interwoven with a story of how baseball has impacted my

3

relationship with my son Ray (primarily the two years I managed his Little League teams). As soon as he was old enough to hold a plastic bat, I started pitching a wiffle ball to him in our living room — something, I'm sure, millions of fathers have done with their young sons or daughters over the years. Little did I know that Ray would someday become a GIANT Giants fan, and that in his late teens he'd actually work at their new ballpark (now known as AT&T Park) as a member of their security crew.

I remember taking Ray to his first baseball game at Candlestick Park in 1984 when he was three-years-old. Good old Candlestick Park, where you could buy the cheapest bleacher tickets and then move to the box seats along the first or third base lines. No security person ever checked our tickets in the mid-1980s because the Giants weren't faring well in either attendance or the standings (they lost 100 games in 1985).

My son's favorite sport, of course, became baseball. I managed two of his Little League teams and was an assistant coach for three other teams, totaling five seasons of seeing his progression as a baseball player. Ray then entered St. Ignatius College Prep and made the freshman squad as a second baseman, the same position that Robby Thompson, his boyhood hero, had held. He did real well his freshman year. The next year, at the start of the season, Ray swung the bat in a game and his kneecap (patella) came loose. He never played in another high school baseball game.

Ray and I have followed the San Francisco Giants through thick and thin over the years. The Giants and baseball have bonded us like glue in the past and will continue to bond us for the remainder of our lives.

Wednesday, June 2, 2010

The Giants lost in the eleventh inning last night. Too bad, because Barry Zito, whose curveball was working like magic for him, pitched a great game through seven innings. Final score: Colorado 2, Giants 1. Two losses in a row to a visiting team is not a good sign. Out of five teams in the West Division, the Giants are in fourth place, trailing first place San Diego by 3 $1/_2$ games, which means they're still within striking distance.

Speaking of Zito and curveballs, it was a curve that hit me in the head in batting practice at Fairfax High that ended my baseball career. I was 15-years-old and hadn't seen many curves up until that time. All I saw was the ball coming at me and I didn't get out of the way in time. Bam! Right above my left ear. I dropped to the ground. My coach and teammates surrounded me. We didn't have batter's helmets in the spring of 1956. Little did I know what the future held in store for me as I lay on the ground.

The next day, I was standing in the same batter's box facing a redheaded pitcher from Hollywood High, Fairfax's crosstown rival. That damn pitcher kept throwing me curveballs the whole game and I ended up striking out five times.

Before our next game, because coach Marty Biegel wouldn't start me, I had some heated words with him. I wanted to start at shortstop, to gain my confidence back, but he wouldn't listen to me, and probably rightfully so. "If you don't start me today," I demanded, "then I'm walking off this field." Coach Biegel replied, "Sit down, Sutton, and be patient."

I walked off the field, never to play another hardball game in my life.

Whatever happened that day happened; I couldn't change it. Instead of concentrating on baseball, the sport in which I thought I had the greatest potential, I devoted myself to football. Since no college recruited me out of high school, I went to Los Angeles Valley Junior College. After playing two seasons at Valley, four colleges offered me a football scholarship. I chose the University of Oregon.

"I'm so happy, Dad," Ray said to me. "I learned how to read today."

"Great — that's great, Son."

"Instead of you reading to me tonight, can I read to you?"

"Of course," I said.

Ray was six-years-old and in the first grade.

He had actually crossed the barrier from non-reader to reader that very day. He was exploding with pride. "Dad, before I read, I want to tell you something else that happened today."

"Sure, what is it?""

"After school we had a baseball game. The other team was ahead until our side had last at bat. Ben and Steve got on base, and then Eric got a hit to tie the score. I was next up, and guess what I did? I hit a home run and we won the game. Everyone patted me on the back and gave me high-fives. I really felt good."

"I'm so proud of you for learning how to read and for becoming a baseball hero," I said before I kissed my son on the cheek and gave him a mighty hug.

Sunday, June 6, 2010

I just finished watching the Giants win a ten-inning game against Pittsburgh 6 – 5. The Pirates tied the game 5 – 5 in the bottom of the ninth on a two-run homer, but the Giants came right back in the top of the tenth when Freddy Sanchez hit a sacrifice fly that scored Andres Torres.

I love my son, I love baseball and I love teaching. I can't think of a better way to spend my time than to manage Ray's Little League team this year.

10

Tuesday, June 8, 2010

As I write this very moment, the Giants are playing the Cincinnati Reds in Cincinnati. The Giants are leading 3 – 0. It's two outs and Matt Cain is still pitching in the bottom of the ninth. "There's only been one run scored against Cain in 33 innings," I hear radio announcer Jon Miller say. Cain must be digging deep into his heart and soul, because I believe he wants to show the world that he's the best pitcher in the majors this year. The game just ended, the Giants winning 3 – 0. Cain has pitched his second complete shutout in a row.

The Giants are on a roll! They've won five of their last six games. They're not going through their usual June swoon. Marvin Gaye once sang, "Will my ball club win the pennant, do you think they have a chance?" Well, my ball club is surely in the pennant race and has a chance. They've played 57 games and they're $2^1/_2$ games out of first place. As long as they're in contention, I'm a happy man.

I'm nervous about managing Little Leaguers. I've never coached a team in my life. What am I going to say to the boys before our first practice? Will I have patience with them? Do I know enough baseball to teach them the game? Should I give them a goal to strive for? The only thing I know is, we have to hustle and work together as a team. If we're successful we'll really have a good time. When the Giants, 49ers and Warriors win, they have a good time. "A good team works and plays together," is what I'll tell them. "Let's help each other as much as we can. Teamwork and hustle — these are the two most important ingredients for a successful season."

Sunday, June 13, 2010

After playing 62 games, the Giants are $1^1/_2$ games out of first place. There are 100 more games left to play. They're in the hunt and getting better as each day passes. Since the season began there have been six position changes. Andres Torres has replaced Aaron Rowand in center field. Buster Posey has come up from the minors to play first base. Aubrey Huff has moved from first base to right field, replacing Nate Schierholtz. Juan Uribe has moved from second base to shortstop, taking over for the injured Edgar Renteria. Freddy Sanchez has come off the disabled list and is now playing second base. Power hitter Pat Burrell has just signed with the team to play left field. The Giants are starting to make their move. Matt Cain is coming into his own. Barry Zito, thank goodness, is pitching well for the first time since he signed with the Giants three years ago. Tim Lincecum was in a funk for three games and it seems like he's broken out of it. Brian Wilson is becoming a force in closing out games.

For the first time since the Barry Bonds era, the Giants seem like they have a chance to win the pennant. Will they be able to do it? I'm surely no great prognosticator, but it looks like it's going to be an exciting race to the finish.

As a Little League coach, I'm going to treat everyone the same. If someone hustles, he'll get positive feedback. If someone lazes around or doesn't give a hoot as to what's going on, then that kid is going to hear it from me.

Tuesday, June 15, 2010

The Giants are hot. They're a half game out of first place. One win for them and a loss for San Diego will put them in the driver's seat.

Managing Little Leaguers can be so frustrating.

Saturday, June 19, 2010

The Giants are playing the Blue Jays in Toronto. They're losing 3-0 in the ninth inning, plus they lost last night to the Jays. Matt Cain, our best pitcher at this point in the season, will take the loss if they lose today. I'm listening to the radio that's in the kitchen, about 30 feet from where I sit at my desk. The Giants are still one game out of first place. They've had a chance to take over first for about a week, but then they lose a game when they're right on the cusp of taking it.

They just lost. Damn.

God, this Little League business is like a roller-coaster ride.

Ray struck out today and started crying.

As a father I feel so deeply for my son. I want so much for his self-esteem to rise.

Saturday, June 26, 2010

I'm sitting in the living room watching the Giants play the Boston Red Sox. It's the bottom of the seventh. The Giants are losing 4 – 2 but threatening. There are no outs and Freddy Sanchez is on second. My favorite Giant, Andres Torres, is at bat. Boston's pitcher sets, glances at Sanchez slowly taking a lead off second, he pitches — and Andres strikes out.

As I'm watching the game, my wife Joan is preparing dinner in the kitchen. Just for fun I ask her, "Tell me, Joan, what is your sexual fantasy?"

"I see myself at a country inn," she says, "in bed with you. It's morning, the weather is warm and you put your arm around me and start kissing me."

"That's exactly what I was thinking — in bed with you somewhere out of town!"

It's true. I really was thinking that.

The Giants lost.

Yesterday wasn't our day. It was as if the whole team woke up on the wrong side of the bed. We stunk! The Anchors sunk us 11 – 3.

Here's a quote I came across on Fatherhood: "Don't be the man you wish you should be, be the father you wish you had had."

Sunday, June 27, 2010

The Giants have lost two games in a row. They're $4\frac{1}{2}$ games behind those immovable Padres who refuse to relinquish first place. Baseball people say a team has to have at least one losing streak during the season. The Giants are still waiting for that to happen to the Padres.

Saturday, July 3, 2010

I watched a film last night on TV. It was a quiet, slow-moving film made especially for HBO called *Sugar*, which focused on a Dominican teenager with a great curveball who was being groomed to become a professional baseball player. It showed what it's like to be Latin with baseball talent and what young men have to go through (especially learning how to speak English in a Dominican baseball boot-camp) to break into the minors and possibly the majors. It takes talent, fortitude, determination, perseverance and luck to reach the majors.

Miguel "Sugar" Santos didn't even finish one season with a Class-A minor league team. He quit and went to New York to look for any job he could find.

It reminded me of my time at the University of Oregon where I injured my knee early on as a running back, which led to my demise as a college football player. It was demeaning to sit on the bench on Saturday afternoons in front of large crowds. It would have been nice to have carried the ball and scored touchdowns and gotten cheers for it, but, as things sometimes happen, it turned out to be a blessing in disguise.

If I had played more often at Oregon, my body and brain would have taken a great toll in the violent sport of college football. Thank goodness I'm still intact. I'm still able, on the eve of my 70th birthday, to walk without pain, but most importantly, I'm able to think straight and coherently.

The Giants have lost **SEVEN** games in a row and are eight games out of first place. Question: How can they be on such a terrible losing streak? Answer: This occasionally happens during a long baseball season.

It's the end of my first year of managing Little Leaguers. We barely missed getting into the playoffs, but the boys can still hold their heads high. I saw great improvement in the team as the season progressed. They all hustled as much as they possibly could. They made mistakes galore but gave their all. This baseball season was like life — with its ups and downs, its good streaks and bad.

My son Ray,
a GIANT
Giants fan.

22

Thursday, July 8, 2010

The Giants won four straight games in Milwaukee this week. I hope they can keep the streak going. They're now five games behind San Diego, a team that was picked to come in last in the West Division. The Rockies and Dodgers are three and four games out, respectively. At least the Giants' bats are starting to come alive. Their pitching is a little wobbly at present. There's no stopping them if they can combine good pitching with good hitting, which is the universal formula for a winning base-ball team. The Giants haven't hit their stride yet. They're an up and down team. A week ago against the Dodgers they lost three home games. I gave up on them when that happened. But now they're winning and I'm with them and

23

rooting for them as I sit at my desk listening to the games. There's nothing like baseball on radio. All four announcers — Jon Miller, Dave Fleming, Duane Kuiper and Mike Krukow — make every game so interesting. All four are knowledgeable, humorous and descriptive. It's a pleasure listening to them.

The greatest hit of my life was when I struck out. It was at Bancroft Junior High's annual All-Star baseball game in 1955. The whole student body was looking on that day, all 2000 of them. I was standing at home plate, my adrenaline rushing, when Chuck Lewman wound up and released the ball, which looked like a balloon to me. My bat met the ball squarely and the ball went higher and farther than any ball I'd ever hit. It was near the foul line, though. I stood at home plate just like Carlton Fisk of the Boston

Red Sox did when he hit a home run close to the foul line in the 1975 World Series against Cincinnati. I watched the ball's flight, motioning and pleading for it to stay fair, just like Fisk did twenty years later.

And guess what? The umpire called it a fair ball.

I blissfully made my way around the bases. When I touched home plate my teammates swarmed around me, picked me up and carried me to our bench. What a feeling! I was literally on top of the world.

But Mr. Frick, the Boys' Vice Principal, walked up to the umpire and told him my home run was a foul ball. Neither the umpire, my coach, nor I thought of challenging the Vice Principal, who was only a spectator at the game like everyone else. But it was the 1950s. **DON'T QUESTION AUTHORITY** symbolized the decade.

I returned to the batter's box intent on duplicating my fabulous feat. Instead, I whiffed at the next two pitches and struck out.

Sunday, July 11, 2010

Sunday is a day of leisure for me. After getting out of bed late, I brew a cup of coffee, cut up an apple and banana, add them to a bowl of corn flakes and start eating while I simultaneously read the *New York Times* and the *Chronicle* and listen to the pre-game radio shows of Mychael Urban and Marty Lurie, two men who are extremely knowledgeable about the Giants and baseball. Before I get to the *Chronicle's* sports section and comics, I read the *Times' Book Review* and columnists Frank Rich, Thomas L. Freidman and Maureen Dowd.

After breakfast, I get to my desk and listen to the game on radio as I'm working on a story or book.

Today I watched most of the World Cup soccer championship match between Spain and the Netherlands. The score was 0 – 0 after regulation play. Spain threatened to score many times, while the Dutch, with little offensive punch, thought that playing dirty defense would help them win the championship. The man who scored the winning goal for Spain in overtime, Andres Iniesta, will probably be a national hero for the remainder of his life.

The Giants beat the Nationals in Washington today 6 – 2. It was their seventh win out of eleven road games before the All-Star break. It's a great achievement to win that many games on the road. They are now four games out of first place. More importantly, they're alive and kicking!

*This is the beginning of my second year of managing Ray's Little League team. I feel so competitive that it's oozing out of me. I want to be the **BEST** manager. I want our team to be the **BEST** in the league. I want my son to experience a year he'll never forget.*

Sunday, July 18, 2010

After my wife Joan and I got home today, I watched the end of the Giants-Mets game. The Giants came from behind in the ninth to tie the score and actually went ahead by a run, but the umpire called the sliding Travis Ishikawa out at home plate when he was obviously safe from every camera angle. The Mets scored the winning run in the bottom of the tenth. Boy, what a tough loss that was!

Little League.
Confidence. Momentum.
A team that works as a TEAM.
It starts now.

Sunday, July 25, 2010

Joan and I are about to leave Nevada City, located in the foothills of the Sierra Nevadas, to drive back to the cool of San Francisco. It's 95 degrees up here, the sky is blue and the air is clean. Because Joan was a former storyteller, we attended the Sierra Storytelling Festival Friday night and all day Saturday. The drive back shouldn't take more than a few hours.

I wonder how the Giants fared yesterday. I hope they won. The last I read, they were right behind San Diego, a team that won't budge from first place. Every sports writer and analyst predicted they would end up at the bottom of the division, but they're still clinging to first. They're going to be hard to overtake.

Joan told me a story about Ray before he left for school this morning. She said he was sitting at the piano with his head down. "What are you doing, Ray?" "I'm praying." "About what?" "That it doesn't rain today." "This is the fifth year of the drought," she said, "don't you know we need rain?" "I know, Mom, but we have our first baseball game today."

"Like father, like son," she said to me.

I think we have the makings of a championship team.

Monday, July 26, 2010

While driving back from Nevada City yesterday, Joan and I were listening to the Giants-Diamondbacks game. Tim Lincecum wasn't having his best day, but he was keeping the Giants in the game. When nearing the Sacramento area on a 95-degree afternoon, we came to an almost complete stop in the worst traffic jam I've ever been in. We were barely crawling along as the Giants were losing 2 – 1. Listening to the game was my only solace. "The Giants better win this one," I told Joan. "If they don't, I'm going to go out of my mind with this traffic and heat."

After the Giants tied it up in the top of the ninth, Sergio Romo replaced Lincecum. Romo got the first batter out, but then the D'backs loaded the bases on him, scaring the daylights out of me and probably every Giants fan. I kept saying to myself, "Don't lose this game, Giants. Make me smile about one thing in the worst traffic jam of my life." Romo miraculously escaped disaster by striking out the last two batters.

The cause of the congestion was the traffic returning to the Bay Area from the Lake Tahoe area. All told, it took us six hours to travel a total of 125 miles.

The Giants won 3 – 2! Buster Posey hit his second double of the game in the tenth (his fourth hit of the day). He was replaced by pinch runner Eli Whiteside who scored easily on Travis Ishikawa's single. Posey is batting .479 in the month of July to raise his average to .371. He's hit in 18 consecutive games. He's the first rookie since Orlando Cepeda to have that long of a hitting streak. Willie McCovey holds the Giants' rookie record of 22 games. Posey is so good that I think he's destined for the Hall of Fame, just like Cepeda and McCovey were before him.

Brian Wilson pitched a perfect tenth inning for his 29th save in 31 chances. It was the Giants' 16th win in 20 games. They trail San Diego by three games.

Compared to his first year in Little League, Ray is hitting the ball much better. He's also surprised me with his pitching. I always thought his arm was weak, but it isn't. It was his continual insistence — "Let me pitch, Dad, let me pitch" — that made me change my mind. The kid hasn't had a run scored on him in two regular season games and his fielding has been flawless at second base.

Tuesday, August 3, 2010

The Giants blanked the Rockies 10 – 0 for their fourth straight win tonight. I love it. They are now two games in back of the Padres. Every team, no matter how high in the standings, hits the skids somewhere along the line. The Padres are due.

Why are the Giants doing so well? They have rookie sensation Buster Posey catching. Benjie Molina, the Giants' catcher for the past $3\frac{1}{2}$ years, has been traded to the Texas Rangers. They have Aubrey Huff, the enthusiastic veteran first baseman, batting .309. They have Andres Torres, a terror in center field, on the base paths and with his bat. They have the very capable pitching staff of Tim Lincecum, Jonathon Sanchez, Matt Cain, Barry Zito and their new young lefty just up from the minors, Madison Bumgarner. They have steady Freddy

Sanchez at second base. They have two reliable veterans, Juan Uribe and Edgar Renteria, sharing shortstop duties. And they have slugger Pat "The Bat" Burrell in left field. There's the leadership of Uribe, Renteria, Burrell and Huff that has made the team's chemistry jell. There's the spirit of Huff and the consistency of Posey. And we mustn't forget manager Bruce Bochy and his coaching staff. The Giants are on the right track with their talent, spirit and leadership. The only blemish is "the Panda," Pablo Sandoval, who's not hitting or fielding as well as last year because he's gained so much weight and looks like a balloon.

Giving the boys an hour of batting practice before each game is probably the most important thing I've learned as a manager this year. If major league teams have batting practice before each game, why shouldn't our Little League team do the same?

Saturday, August 7, 2010

The Giants are one game out of first place with two months remaining in this marathon of a baseball season.

Today I watched seven men join the football greats at pro football's Hall of Fame in Canton, Ohio. Jerry Rice (Wide receiver, San Francisco 49er), who ran as swiftly as a deer and could catch any ball thrown his way, let it be known in his acceptance speech that his success came mainly from a fear of failing. Other members of the class of 2010 are: Emmitt Smith (Running back, Dallas Cowboys), Floyd Little (Running back, Denver Broncos), Russ Grimm (Offensive guard, Washington Redskins), Dick LeBeau (Defensive back, Detroit Lions), along with Rickey Jackson (Linebacker, New Orleans Saints) and John Randle (Defensive tackle,

Minnesota Vikings). These men are our modern day Greek Olympians or Roman gladiators, whichever way you want to look at it, who will forever be memorialized in the Football Hall of Fame. It was a distinction that I once sought but didn't come anywhere near to gaining.

Max Coley, my backfield coach at the University of Oregon, yelled at me in front of the whole team on a hot summer day that turned out to be my death knell as a football player, although I persevered for two years with the hope of breaking into Oregon's lineup. Oh, I played miniscule minutes against Washington, Stanford, Michigan and Arizona, but that was it. When Max called me to enter our team's first scrimmage that summer, I just stood on the sideline and shook my head. That's when he went ballistic and shouted for everyone on the field to hear: "Sutton, you'll never play for Oregon as long as I'm coaching here!" I refused to enter the scrimmage because I saw my future before me: a badly mangled right knee. Two days earlier I had wrenched my knee in a football drill and had to be carried off the field. I overslept the morning of the scrimmage and got to the training room to find that the trainer and all the coaches and players were out on the field. Not one person was there to help me tape my weak, sore and swollen right knee. I don't know why I did it, but I suited up without taping it.

If I hadn't injured my knee early on at Oregon I might have gotten more playing time. Because I woke up late and didn't tape it, that, in a nutshell, was the end of my football career. I sometimes wonder what would have happened if I had quit the football team. I can only surmise that I wouldn't be what I am today: a person who sticks to something until he finishes it.

Monday, August 9, 2010

The Giants are two games behind the Padres after a two-win, four-loss road trip.

The Hornets stung us today 14 – 13. Ray pitched one inning and had seven runs scored on him. He was getting hit so hard he was crying for me to take him out. I called a time-out, walked to the mound and told him he was going to finish the inning.

41

Friday, August 13, 2010

The Padres just beat the Giants 3 – 2 for
their fifth straight victory, making a fool of
today's losing pitcher Jonathan Sanchez, who
guaranteed that the Giants would sweep the
three-game series. San Diego is now $3^1/_2$ games
up on us.

*We played the no-win, eleven-loss Lions
today and barely squeaked by with an 8 – 7
win.*

*Ray lost it today. He wanted to pitch two
innings when I only wanted him to pitch one.
I had a talk with him after the game. I said,
"There's only one manager on this team.
When I took you out after pitching one inning,
you argued with me. You cause dissension on
the team when you argue and cry and think*

only of yourself. I won't tolerate this kind of behavior, Son."

He said, "I'm sorry, Dad," and I could see he meant it.

Saturday, August 14, 2010

The Giants won a very tight, intense game against the Padres today. It was nip and tuck into the eleventh inning with the score tied 2 – 2. The Giants were at bat and Buster Posey hit a ground ball up the middle. The Padres' shortstop and second baseman almost collided going for the ball and neither of them, for a split second, knew where the ball was. By the time one of them picked it up, Buster was sliding head-first into second. What a heads-up, clutch play by Posey! The kid is only 23-years-old. He's a born winner. He can bat for a high average, he's a home run threat, he can call a good game from behind the plate and he has a cannon of an arm to throw out base stealers. As an extra bonus, he's much faster than our previous catcher, Benjie Molina. The kid is priceless. He scored the winning run. The Giants are $2\frac{1}{2}$ games out.

The boys are jelling into a fine team. They're beginning to realize that they can stand up to any team we face. They're finding out that awareness, hustle and playing aggressive baseball can do wonders for their confidence.

Tuesday, August 17, 2010

The Giants are again four games out of first place. They lost the weekend series to the Padres 2 games to 1. The Padres beat the Cubs today at home while the Giants were traveling to Philadelphia. Tim Lincecum is having pitching problems. He's getting hit badly and can't last more than four or five innings. Something is wrong with "The Freak."

Ray struck out yesterday and shook it off like rain off an umbrella. I was more proud of him for doing that than getting three hits and making four flawless plays at second base. He's starting to mature.

Sunday, August 22, 2010

The Giants seem slower, weaker and tired this week. They lost four of six games in Philadelphia and St. Louis, two cities where the humidity and heat must kill West Coast teams.  They got clobbered 8 – 0 in the final game of the road trip against St. Louis. Barry Zito didn't get past the fourth inning! Just by listening to the game on radio, I could sense they gave up against St. Louis. Today's winning pitcher for the Cardinals threw only 86 pitches. An average pitcher throws 100 pitches in six or seven innings! In other words, the Cardinals' pitcher mowed us down. Why? Heat and humidity is my theory.

Last week the Giants were one game behind San Diego. Today they're six games out. It's summer throughout the United States except for San Francisco. Our city is a natural air conditioner during the summer. I know the Giants aren't going to give up, though. They were just tired, beat and bushed today.

Ray told me he learned something today. He said he talked to himself out on the mound when the bases were loaded. "No one's on base and I'm going to throw strikes," is what he said to himself. This was a great leap of faith for him. He was thinking positive and found out that it really works.

Wednesday, September 1, 2010

Colorado beat the Giants 2 – 1 Monday night. The Giants came back last night and won 5 – 2. Tim Lincecum, who hadn't won a game since July 30th, has returned to his old form and pitched eight solid innings tonight to lead the Giants to a 2 – 1 squeaker over Rockies' pitching ace Ubaldo Jimenez. As Giants' announcer Duane Kuiper would say, "This is torture!" Brian Wilson pitched a perfect ninth inning for his league-leading 38th save in 42 chances. This off-the-wall, black-bearded wonder who thirsts for save situations is turning into a superstar before our eyes. The Giants are now three games in back of San Diego.

This past weekend I drove down to L.A. to attend our annual junior high/high school baseball reunion. I wrote a poem about it yesterday.

THE LAST SUNDAY IN AUGUST

*The last Sunday in August has become a tradition.
It's when coach Louie Ryave's
junior high baseball teams from the early '50s
meet at Rancho Park on Pico and Motor.*

*All of Louie's boys are now in their late 60s
or early 70s.
It's a day of hot sun, green grass, bats, balls,
mitts, gloves, hitting, fielding and talking.*

*There was Tommy, Lenny, Alan, Vic, Ronnie,
Davie, Billy, Jimmy, Max, Stan, Stuffy, Bobby,
Moe, Roland, Marc, Freddy, Richard, Larry,
Louie, Gerson, Mike and Teddy.*

After the game that nobody knows or cares
who won,
we all had a Pink's hot dog or two or three,
with chili,
caught up on each other's lives
and reminisced about the good old days
at Bancroft Junior High and Fairfax High.

It's a day of feeling young again,
a day that always turns out to be the best
Sunday of the year.

— Joseph Sutton

Saturday, September 4, 2010

The Giants were down 4 – 0 to the Dodgers when I gave up on them in the sixth inning and changed channels. When I turned back to the game, which was over by then, San Francisco's four announcers were picking their most valuable player of the game. I was completely taken aback to find out that the Giants had beaten the Dodgers 5 – 4. Buster Posey, Edgar Renteria and Pat Burrell each hit one-run home runs, and in the bottom of the ninth, Juan Uribe hit a two-run homer to end the game. Damn, I missed a great comeback.

I've learned my lesson: You can't count the Giants out, ever, this season. I'm now convinced that Yogi Berra was right: "It ain't over till it's over."

The Giants are now two games out of first place because the Padres have lost nine games in a row. Everyone predicted they would hit a bump in the road, but who woulda thunk it would be a nine-game nosedive? There's hope for the Giants with 25 games left to play.

Ray had a good game today. He hit a solid triple into left field to drive in two runs, and he pitched two scoreless innings to save another win for us.

Wednesday, September 8, 2010

The Giants are one game out of first place. San Diego's losing streak ended at 10 games. This race is going to go down to the wire.

We defeated the Spartans 12-4 today. Ray got three hits. He played practically the whole game on a gimpy knee. He hurt it after colliding with the Spartan catcher at home plate in the first inning. He didn't whine about it like he might have last year, but gutted it out the rest of the game.

Sunday, September 12, 2010

The Giants won three of four games, in San Diego, and are now tied with the Padres for first place. They're showing the Padres, as the season is coming to a close, who the boss is. They've won 10 of their last 14 games while the Padres have lost 13 of their last 17. The Giants held San Diego to a total of five runs in the four-game series. I'm in absolute ecstasy right now.

Sunday, September 17, 2010

Barry Zito, with the help of Jose Guillen's bat, won his first game in two months and the Giants have regained first place with a 9 – 2 win over Milwaukee. Guillen hit a grand slam in the first inning and drove in two more runs for a 6 RBI day.

One day the Giants are in first place, the next day it's the Padres. This is *torture, torture, torture!*

Sunday, September 26, 2010

Matt Cain had a no-hitter going against Colorado with one out in the eighth inning, but then Jay Payton beat out an infield hit. Cain struck out the next batter, but then Melvin Mora hit a pinch-hit two-run homer. Those were the only two hits off Cain and the Giants won 4 – 2. They beat the onrushing Rockies 2 games out of 3 and are now one game up on the Padres. Could this be the year of the Giants?

Wednesday, September 29, 2010

The Giants are two games ahead of San Diego with five games remaining. San Diego comes into town Friday. This weekend's three game series will decide the winner of the West Division.

The Giants haven't played a postseason game since 2003, the year they lost to the Florida Marlins. They should have beaten the Marlins in that Division Series. Jose Cruz Jr., in the third game, who was perfection in right field the whole season, dropped an easy fly ball in the bottom of the eleventh inning that my great-grandmother could have caught. I'll never forgive Cruz for that fatal error, because it led to the Marlins scoring the winning run that very same inning. In the next game, to this day, I don't know why manager Felipe Alou left

J.T. Snow on second base with two outs in the ninth inning. J.T., the potential tying run, was slow. My son Ray and I yelled at the TV screen for Alou to replace him with a pinch runner, but he didn't hear us. There was a single to left field by Jeffrey Hammonds and J.T., in a close play at home plate, crashed into catcher Pudge Rodriguez who held onto the ball to end the game and the series. The Marlins beat the Cubs in seven games for the National League pennant and went on to defeat the Yankees 4 games to 2 in the World Series.

Sunday, October 3, 2010

The Giants have just defeated the Padres 3 – 0 to win the West Division by two games. If they had lost they would have tied for the division lead and would have had to travel to San Diego for a one-game tiebreaker to see who was going to play the Atlanta Braves. If the Giants win three games against Atlanta, they'll play for the National League pennant against the winner of the Philadelphia-Cincinnati series. So far, all is right with the baseball gods of San Francisco.

Thursday, October 7, 2010

"The Freak" was right on target tonight and did himself proud in his postseason debut against the Atlanta Braves. He pitched a complete game, struck out 14 Braves, walked one batter and allowed only two hits in game one of the National League Division Series. The game's only run came on Cody Ross' two-out single to left in the fourth inning that brought home Buster Posey from second base.

I couldn't be a happier man than I am right now.

Monday, October 11, 2010

The baseball gods are still with the Giants. They defeated Atlanta 3 games to 1 (all four games decided by one run) and will now face the Philadelphia Phillies to see which team is going to represent the National League in the World Series. The Braves series was extremely tense and exciting, especially when the eighth and ninth innings rolled around. Atlanta's only win came in the second game when they fought back from a three-run deficit to tie the game and send it into extra innings. Rick Ankiel hit the game-winning home run in the top of the eleventh. Poor Brooks Conrad, Atlanta's second baseman, made three crucial errors in game three that cost his team a victory. The Giants won that game 3 – 2, and went on to win game four by the same score. The series might have gone a full five games if it wasn't for Conrad's errors. I wonder if he'll ever be able to show his face in Atlanta again. Those three errors were equivalent to Bill Buckner's error, when a ground ball went through his legs to help the Mets defeat the Red Sox in the 1986 World Series.

Tim Lincecum, who won two of the Giants' three games, was the MVP of the series. Cody Ross, who the Giants acquired on waivers from the Florida Marlins in late August, had the hottest bat in the series. The whole Giants team, celebrating their series win on Atlanta's infield, took time to salute Atlanta's retiring manager Bobby Cox in a splendid display of sportsmanship.

The National League Championship Series with the Phillies begins on Saturday in

Philadelphia. Both teams have great pitching staffs. The Giants have Lincecum, Cain, Jonathan Sanchez and young Madison Bumgarner.

Thank goodness Barry Zito, one of the highest paid pitchers in the majors, was left off the 25-man roster. He just hasn't pitched well since he became a Giant in 2007.

Philadelphia's pitching staff consists of Roy Halladay, Cole Hamels, Roy Oswalt and Joe Blanton. Halladay has pitched two no-hitters this season. It should be quite a series.

The unsung heroes of our championship team are the coaches. They've given so much of their time and energy and have received very little recognition. What they've received, though, is the satisfaction of seeing the boys they've coached gain confidence in themselves.

64

Saturday, October 16, 2010

Game one against Philadelphia is going on as I write.

As Yogi Berra said, "It's deja vu all over again," because Cody Ross has just hit his second home run off of Roy "No Hit" Halladay in the top of the fifth. Halladay's pitch was the same exact pitch, in the same exact spot as Cody's first home run in the third inning. Homer number two, to top it off, landed in almost the same spot as the first — in Philadelphia's left field bleachers. Unbelievable! If this doesn't give the Giants a lift, I don't know what will. The Giants are now leading 2 – 1. Ross has broken Halladay's spell twice in one game, which is unheard of when Roy Halladay is pitching. The Giants now know they have a chance against him, even though he pitched a no-hitter against Cincinnati last week. "We can beat this guy," is what I bet they're saying to themselves in the dugout this very second.

We are now in the sixth inning. Freddy Sanchez, from my hometown of Hollywood, is at bat — and grounds out.

Aubrey Huff — grounds out.

The Buster is at bat. I predict he'll get good wood on the ball — and I was right. It's a solid single to right center.

Pat "The Bat" Burrell stands at home plate. It's two outs — and he doubles off the left field wall. Posey scores from first. 3 – 1. This is great!

Juan Uribe (Ooooo-ree-bay) — follows with another double. 4 – 1 Giants.

LET'S GO GIANTS!!

I've watched every pitch since the Giants played the Padres in the last three games of the regular season to decide the winner of the West Division. That three-game series had the atmosphere of a playoff series, which I believe turned out to be a confidence builder for the Giants. Then came Atlanta and poor Brooks Conrad who made a bunch of errors that thwarted Atlanta's hopes. Now it's the Phillies. God, it would be absolutely glorious to see the Giants in the World Series.

It's the bottom of the sixth.

Chase Utley faces "The Freak." Utley hits a grounder up the middle that Lincecum deflects with his glove. Uribe picks it up but his throw to first is late.

The Phillies' top home run and RBI man, big Ryan Howard, thank goodness, strikes out for the second time against Lincecum.

Jayson Werth is up and barely misses two of Lincecum's pitches. If he tags one, it's gonna go. "Come on, Timmy. Get him out!" Werth connects. Home run. Goddammit.

Lincecum comes back and strikes out Jimmy Rollins.

Raul Ibanez draws a two-out walk.

Carlos Ruiz, who hit a home run off Lincecum his first at bat, thank heaven, strikes out.

Every pitch is so important! Both teams have scored with two outs in the sixth. The Giants are still up 4 – 3.

It's the bottom of the eighth. "The Freak," with a jacket on, remains in the dugout. He's thrown 113 pitches and Bruce Bochy, a magician with his personnel changes, mixing and matching his men to perfection throughout the postseason, replaces Lincecum with Javier Lopez, a lefty sidearmer whose main roll is to get lefties out.

Utley, a lefty, grounds out. Ryan Howard, another lefty, strikes out for the third time. Lopez has done his job.

Brian "Fear the Beard" Wilson replaces Lopez to face the man who hit a two-run homer off Lincecum his last at bat, and Jayson Werth singles. The next batter, Jimmy Rollins, strikes out.

The Giants loaded the bases in the top of the ninth but didn't score. It's still 4 – 3, Giants. Three more outs to go.

Brian Wilson faces Raul Ibanez — and strikes him out. *One.*

Carlos Ruiz is hit by a pitch.

This is absolute torture for me.

Pinch hitter Ross Gload — strikes out swinging. *Two.*

Shane Victorino swings at a 3 – 2 pitch. *Three*!!

Yippee!!

Did we learn anything? I think we did. We learned that preparation is key. If you're prepared you'll do better than you ever thought possible.

My cousin Vic called tonight and put the season in perspective for me. He said, "Joe, you wanted to manage so you could help Ray with his self-esteem. Guess what? You helped. I don't think I've ever seen him more confident of himself. I'm proud of both of you."

Sunday, October 17, 2010

The Giants lost game two to the Phillies 6 – 1. The only bright spot for the Giants was Cody Ross, who hit his third home run of the National League Championship Series. Last night he broke up a no-hitter against Roy Halladay in the third inning. Tonight he did the same thing against Roy Oswalt in the fifth inning. The series is tied one game apiece. The Giants are coming home for the next three games.

My son is my closest friend. We go to Giants games and watch sporting events on TV. Whenever we're together, I try to teach him the virtues of honesty, responsibility and fairness, while he teaches me to keep my big mouth shut.

Someday, when I look back, I'll smile and say to myself, "Those were the days. We were a great team, Ray and I. Boy, am I glad I had a chance to be a father."

Wednesday, October 20, 2010

It's a thrill watching the Giants.

Last night Matt Cain pitched seven strong innings and the Giants won game three against the Phillies 3 – 0.

Game four was a tug of war, an ebb and flow game. The Giants won it in the bottom of the ninth 6 – 5 when Juan Uribe hit a sacrifice fly to left field that brought in Aubrey Huff from third base. Buster "The Real Hero of the Night" Posey set it up with his fourth hit of the game, a double, that got Huff to third. By the way, the Giants have won almost 70% of their games since Huff started wearing a red "rally thong" around the clubhouse in late August.

The Giants lead the series 3 games to 1.

Thursday, October 21, 2010

The Giants are in the catbird seat. All they have to do is win one of three more games against Philadelphia and they'll go to the World Series and probably play the Texas Rangers, that is, if the Rangers beat the Yankees in one of two games on their home field.

The whole Bay Area will go crazy if the Giants win tonight. The two best pitchers in baseball are facing each other: Lincecum versus Halladay.

The postseason is where every pitch, every inch, every player counts. Last night, everyone who played for the Giants contributed to the win. But one player stood out above all the rest, and that was Buster Posey, who starred on both offense and defense. Two of his four hits were doubles, and just as important, he made a great play at home plate, catching a one hop throw from Aaron Rowand in center field to tag out a hard charging Carlos Ruiz at home plate.

All I can say right now, three hours before game five, is: **GO GIANTS!!**

Sometimes I wonder if I said the right thing to Ray one day. He was pitching and getting battered in a Little League baseball game. I wanted to teach him a lesson because he was getting down on himself and wanted to quit pitching that day. I walked out to the mound and didn't say, "Don't give up on yourself." Instead, I said, "You're going to pitch till the inning is over." I wonder if he remembers that incident. He was 10 at the time.

Saturday, October 23, 2010

The Giants lost game five 5 – 3. Their defense had one poor inning and the Phillies took advantage of it by scoring three runs. One pitch, one bad inning, one of anything can turn the tide of a game. The Giants looked lackadaisical and made too many mistakes. Hence, a loss.

It's two hours before game six begins in Philadelphia.

My friends Jerry Lipkin, Alan Blum and I have vowed to propel the Giants into the World Series by calling each other on the day of the game and wearing our Giants caps while watching the game. If doom is looking the Giants in the face, we turn the bill of our caps 90 degrees to the right.

9:30 p.m.

The Giants have won the National League Pennant four times in the 52 years they've been in San Francisco: 1962, 1989, 2002 and now 2010. It was a real nail-biter tonight. In the eighth inning, the score tied 2 – 2 with two outs, Juan Uribe, with a count of no balls and two strikes on him, hit a solo home run that barely cleared Philadelphia's right field wall. The Giants won 3 – 2 and took the series 4 games to 2. Ooooo-ree-bay has done it again.

The whole team, in fact, has done it again: Cody Ross, Aubrey Huff, Buster Posey, Andres Torres, Freddy Sanchez, Jeremy Affeldt, Madison Bumgarner, Edgar Renteria, Pat Burrell, Tim Lincecum, Matt Cain, Jonathan Sanchez, Nate Schierholtz, Travis Ishikawa, Mike Fontenot, Pablo Sandoval, Javier Lopez, Santiago Casilla, Ramon Ramirez,

Eli Whiteside, Sergio Romo, Guillermo Mota,
Aaron Rowand, and none other than the Giants'
tenacious closer, Brian Wilson, who struck out
big, powerful Ryan Howard looking at a third
strike with two men on base for the final out.

I feel compelled to quote the closing lines of
Ernest Lawrence Thayer's *"Casey at the Bat"*:

*Oh, somewhere in this favored land the sun
[in San Francisco] is shining bright;*

*The band is playing somewhere, and somewhere
hearts are light,*

*And somewhere men are laughing, and somewhere
children shout;*

*But there is no joy in Mudville [or Philadelphia]
— mighty Casey [Ryan Howard] has struck out.*

The Giants win the pennant!

The Giants win the pennant!

The Giants win the pennant because Jerry, Alan and I turned the bills of our caps to the right when Ryan Howard was at bat!

Next up: the Texas Rangers.

Thursday, October 28, 2010

It's Joan's and my 31st anniversary today. I'm about to leave the house to attend her two-hour, once-a-week class at San Francisco State called "Close Encounters with Six Greek Gods." After class, and Joan thoroughly understands why, I'll be driving to the East Bay to watch the second World Series game with my poker group, The Royal Flush. We might even get to play some poker after the game.

The Giants won the opening game of the World Series last night against the Rangers 11 – 7. All their hits seemed like doubles, with Freddy Sanchez hitting three in a row. There was a three-run homer by none other than Juan "Clutch" Ooooo-ree-bay. Tim Lincecum pitched only a fair game. Everyone who played, as usual, contributed.

Here's hoping Matt Cain pitches a great game tonight. Texas is a potent hitting team. A pitcher can't relax for a minute against them.

12:30 a.m.

The Giants won the second game of the Series 9 – 0. As Giants' announcer Mike Krukow sometimes says, "It was a laugher." It was a tight game (2 – 0 in favor of the Giants) until the eighth inning. In that inning the Giants scored seven runs, as three Texas relievers couldn't get the ball over the plate and walked four batters. The Giants got only two hits that inning, one being a bases-loaded triple by Aaron Rowand. In the fifth inning, the score 0 – 0, Ian Kinsler of the Rangers smashed a ball that hit the top of the padded center field wall for what seemed like a home run — but the ball, miraculously, bounced back of its own accord for a double. That apparent home run could have changed the whole complexion of the game, but somehow the baseball gods were on San Francisco's side tonight. Matt Cain, who hasn't been scored upon in three postseason games, pitched $7\frac{1}{3}$ scoreless innings before the bullpen took over.

The Giants are a bunch of unknowns who are two victories shy of winning the 2010 World Series. It would be the first time they've won the Fall Classic since moving from the Bronx to San Francisco in 1958. The people of San Francisco, after waiting 52 years, are starving for a title. They are now on the brink of gaining it.

No one on the team, outside of Tim Lincecum, is known in the baseball world. They have no superstars like Barry Bonds, Willie

Mays, Derek Jeter, Ryan Howard, Josh Hamilton, Albert Pujols or Alex Rodriguez. This team of no-names is a bunch of fighters and scrappers. They don't give up. They're tenacious. They're like your average Joe in any profession, but somehow they have blended together to become a **TEAM**. Destiny is on their side.

Sunday, October 31, 2010

What can I say? This is the year of the Giants. They won their third game tonight in Texas. They're leading the Series 3 games to 1. Texas won last night 4 – 2. Tonight a 21-year-old rookie pitcher from North Carolina, Madison Bumgarner, pitched eight scoreless innings. The Rangers got only three hits off him. Brian Wilson came in to finish them off one, two, three in the ninth and the Giants won 4 – 0. If the Giants win game five with Tim Lincecum tomorrow, this city will go crazy.

"You have many good qualities, Ray. Four of them shine brightly in my eyes. One, you are gentle. Two, you are sensitive. Three, you are intelligent. And the fourth quality you possess is your daring. I first noticed your

*daring when you were playing baseball —
more specifically, when you were on the base
paths. I saw that you were taking chances
and experimenting. I want you to continue
doing this. Live your life as it was meant to be
lived — experimenting, creating, being adven-
turous, bold and daring. Don't ever let me or
anyone else suffocate you in this endeavor.
Always be that daring young man that I know
you are."*

Wednesday, November 3, 2010

Where do I begin? Two days ago? Today? Does it matter that the Giants won the World Series in five games? Does it matter that they won the last game 3 − 1 on Edgar Renteria's three-run home run in the top of the seventh? Of course it does. But today, my son Ray and I went to the Giants' victory parade where it was estimated that over a million people attended. This is what a World Series championship brings to a city: a stream of joy, celebration and togetherness.

Ray and I boarded a very crowded Muni streetcar at West Portal station. A man decked out in the Giants' colors of orange and black, along with an orange cape and an orange and black striped stovepipe hat, had an accordion and played "Take Me Out to the Ballgame" as we started out from each station. All of us in the packed car sang to his accompaniment. This is what the whole day was about: bringing people together to celebrate the San Francisco Giants.

Ray and I got off at Civic Center station and walked up the stairs to street level to come upon a mass of people, all of them wearing something Giants: caps, T-shirts or jerseys. The T-shirts had everything from "World Series Champions" to Brian Wilson's face with a beard to "Torture" to what Tim Lincecum said to a TV interviewer — "Fuck Yeah." Both my son and I were wearing his homemade orange "Croix de Candlestick" T-shirts.

Before the parade began, we were standing on a very crowded sidewalk along the parade route. People were so happy the Giants were finally world champions that they were cheering at empty buses that passed through the route.

A man on the roof of a building, waving a huge Giants flag, had people cheering for ten minutes. Standing on a crowded sidewalk on an unusually hot November day was a little uncomfortable. Luckily, for Ray and me, the janitor of a building we were standing in front of, let us inside to take an elevator to the second floor so we could get a better view of the parade. For this good deed, Ray gave him one of his T-shirts. About a dozen other people were up there with us.

And then the parade began. Motorized cable cars with the ballplayers in them passed by and everyone cheered their lungs out. Every player must have felt like they were in paradise with such thunderous adulation. Former San Francisco heroes Willie Mays, Willie McCovey and

Juan Marichal passed by in open convertibles. The same with the Giants' announcers Mike Krukow, Duane Kuiper, Jon Miller and Dave Fleming. It was Fleming's radio call that I predict will forever be played over and over again as his voice cracked while calling Edgar Renteria's game-winning home run in the fifth game.

The marching bands of the University of California and San Francisco's Riordan High School marched by. Principal owner Bill Neukom, general manager Brian Sabean and team President Larry Baer were cheered. Even the employees of the Giants got hearty cheers. Giants' manager Bruce Bochy, who turned out to be a genius in his postseason decision-making, proudly held the World Series trophy as he rode in a convertible with his wife. I've never heard so much cheering. It was deafening at times. It was the largest crowd I've ever been a part of in my life.

The Giants defeated the Texas Rangers in five games with a starting lineup of unknowns, a team that's been called "castoffs and misfits," a team that truly was a **TEAM**, where their main goal was to win the highest honor a baseball team can earn. It didn't matter if someone played in a game or not — just as long as he thought of the **TEAM** over himself they were going to go all the way.

It was truly a remarkable year for them, always underdogs, never giving up, starting two-out rallies, eking out so many games by one run that it became torture for the team and their fans. You knew the baseball gods were on their side when a sure-fire home run by Ian Kinsler of the Rangers hit the padding on top of the center field wall and came bouncing back to the field of play. That "almost" home run could have changed the whole outcome of the Series. But it was only a double, and that's as far as

Kinsler got that inning. The Giants went on to win four of five games, the last two games outstandingly pitched by Madison Bumgarner and Tim Lincecum. Texas scored a combined 7+0+4+0+1=12 runs in the Series.

San Francisco, on the other hand, scored 11+9+2+4+3=29 runs. Great pitching, great defense, timely hitting and great team chemistry is why they are now the 2010 World Series Champions.

 The Giants did things you never expected: a rookie catcher batting in the middle of the order; an old veteran injured most of the season who became the MVP of the World Series; a 21-year-old rookie pitching a shutout in game four of the World Series; a man who came back 12 days later after having an appendectomy; a man acquired on waivers near the end of the season who

became a postseason hero; a man acquired for a low price in mid-season who won late-inning games with home runs. This ragtag bunch of castoffs, misfits and retreads became world champions. As Mike Krukow said, "It wasn't a team of the best players, it was a team with the best **TEAM**."

That's the year of the Giants, except for one more thing. Jerry Lipkin, Alan Blum and I made a pact that we'd call each other before each game, starting with the first postseason game against Atlanta to the National League Championship Series with the Phillies to the five World Series games to remind each other about wearing our Giants caps during the games and to turn the bill of our caps to the right if the Giants were in trouble. Our superstitious ritual worked!

I'm sure that millions of other Giants fans had their own rituals that helped the team reach the mountaintop of baseball.

I'm going to paraphrase Russ Hodges' call from way back in 1951:

"The Giants win the World Series!!"

"The Giants win the World Series!!"

"The Giants win the World Series!!"

The whole day turned out to be a wonderful bonding experience for Ray and me.

 Today the whole Bay Area had only one thing on its mind, and that was to celebrate the Giants, a team that symbolizes what a team, even a democracy, can accomplish when everyone forgets their own selfish interests and works together to achieve a goal. Maybe I should send a copy of this book to the President and every Representative and Senator in Congress. Our country might be a better place if they followed the Giants' lead.

I choked up when Ray was about to fly the coop for the first time and drive down to attend San Diego State University. We stood outside. We hugged and kissed each other on the cheek. He thanked me for what I've done for him.

Tears are streaming down my face as I sit here and remember my son from the day he entered the world to now. Memories keep popping into my brain and reminding me of those times that will never happen again. His birth, his first sports team (soccer), his first Little League hit, his first touchdown in high school, teaching him to ride a bike and drive a car, the day he told me he could read at the age of six, his bar mitzvah, his first date in high school, going out a multitude of times to pitch baseballs and hit grounders to him, managing two of his baseball teams, reading his creative stories and essays, worrying for him, praying for him, seeing him get down on himself and occasionally getting mad at him because of his negative attitude. All these and so many more memories have entered my mind. I hope and pray that Joan and I have prepared him well. With all my heart, I wish my son the very best on his life's journey.

The Giants Win! The Giants Win!

I am banging cooking pots,
On the porch,
With my four-year-old son;
Smooching my wife;
Sharing throat-clearing hoots along the street;
High-fiving everyone.

Later I will have more drinks,
Than I've had all year.

I'll crash a reading neighbor's pad,
And have another two.

I will talk drunken gibberish,
Hooting,
Waiting for this night to never end.
You know,

I did not hit for them,
Did not pitch for them,
Did not reach over the fence and
pull a flyout into the bleachers for a homer,
Did not make a pitching change,
Did not do the catering;

All I did was watch;

Why does it feel so good?

— Steve Hermanos, from
O, Gigantic Victory!